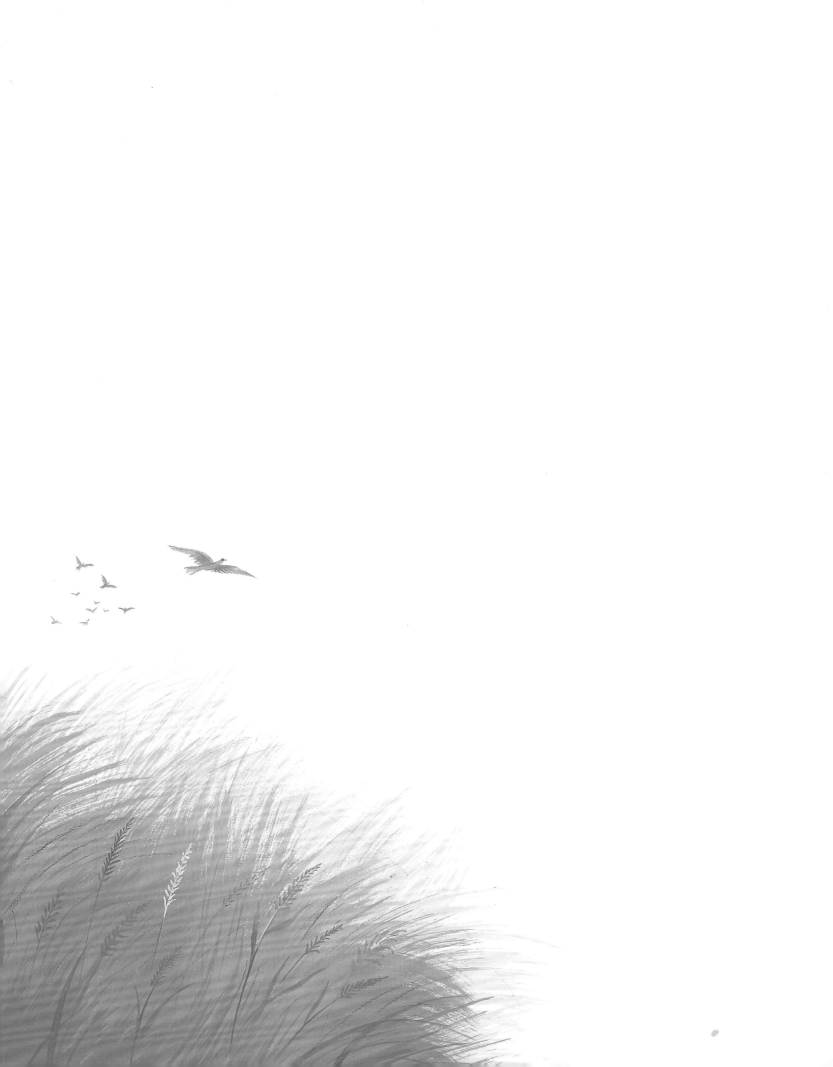

MOZART

Great Names

MOZART

Mason Crest Publishers
Philadelphia

The early morning sunlight danced over the awakening flowers and sleepy leaves of the plants on the balcony, and then slid into the room on a slight puff of wind.

The house it entered was a musician's home. Music flowed through the corridors. Violins, cellos, clarinets, sheets of music, and the like lay about the rooms. There was a harpsichord by the window. A three-year-old boy called Mozart was standing on tiptoes, arms at full stretch, in front of the harpsichord, playing. Inspired by his pure, lively music the sunlight danced.

Born in Salzburg Austria in 1756, Wolfgang Amdadeus Mozart demonstrated his affinity for music early. By the time he

was five, the only thing that could keep him still for any length of time was the music lessons he had with his sister Nannerl. One day, when his father and a friend were taking tea, they noticed the usually active Mozart sitting quietly at a desk, writing with intense concentration in a clumsy hand.

"What are you doing, son?" his father asked.

"Writing music," replied young Mozart seriously. The two men smiled at each other and asked if they could take a look. To their total amazement, on his page of misshapen tadpole-like notes was, in fact, the start of an exceptionally lovely piece of music. Mozart's musician father was so proud and pleased that he nearly cried. He decided that Mozart's genius should be shown to the world.

So the family traveled to Vienna, one of the important musical centers of the day, where Mozart's father set about trying to arrange a performance for the emperor and empress. Finally he succeeded and Mozart, heavily

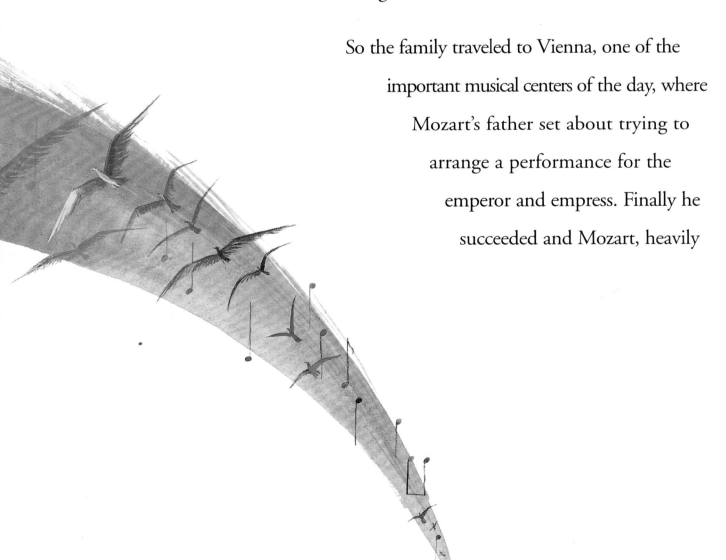

powdered and wearing a wig and formal court dress, was escorted into the palace. As he entered, talk broke out among the assembled lords and ladies.

"Is he really a child prodigy?" they asked.

"He looks very small," they observed.

Yet when he began to play, they could hardly believe their ears. Then the King asked him to play with one finger on a keyboard under a cloth, but Mozart played as accurately and as beautifully as before. He made the cloth seem like a stream beneath which the keys darted around happily like tiny fish.

Mozart's brilliant success in Vienna led his father to organize a longer trip across Europe. With nothing to do except sit for hours in the carriage listening to the sound of the horse's hooves, Mozart began to invent an imaginary kingdom. He was the king on tour of his realm. His sister was his beautiful queen. All the things he passed and left behind were, in fact, the things that waited to greet him. In this way, the long journeys passed without boredom.

Arriving in Paris, Mozart met another king and queen, but he was unimpressed with the lords and ladies of the court who knew little of music and cared for nothing but social position. He would have preferred being in his carriage. At the end of his performances, they presented him with kisses and small gifts rather than money. Worried that their money was running out, Mozart's father decided to move the family to London.

LONDON

They traveled by boat this time, sailing up the River Thames to the Port of London. When Mozart caught sight of the Tower of London, he was so excited that he wanted to rush up on the deck. Unfortunately, he was too seasick to leave his cabin. The sights of the city filled the adventurous young genius with great expectation and, it turned out, the days they spent in London were some of the happiest during his tour.

It was in London that Mozart met his lifelong friend J.C. Bach. J.C. was the son of J.S. Bach and a famous musician like his father. In a performance for the King and Queen, J.C. placed Mozart on his knee and the two of them took turns playing. The music sounded as though the same hands had played it all. J.C. was 30 at the time and Mozart was eight. But music overcame the differences of age and size. It brought them together as equal and as friends.

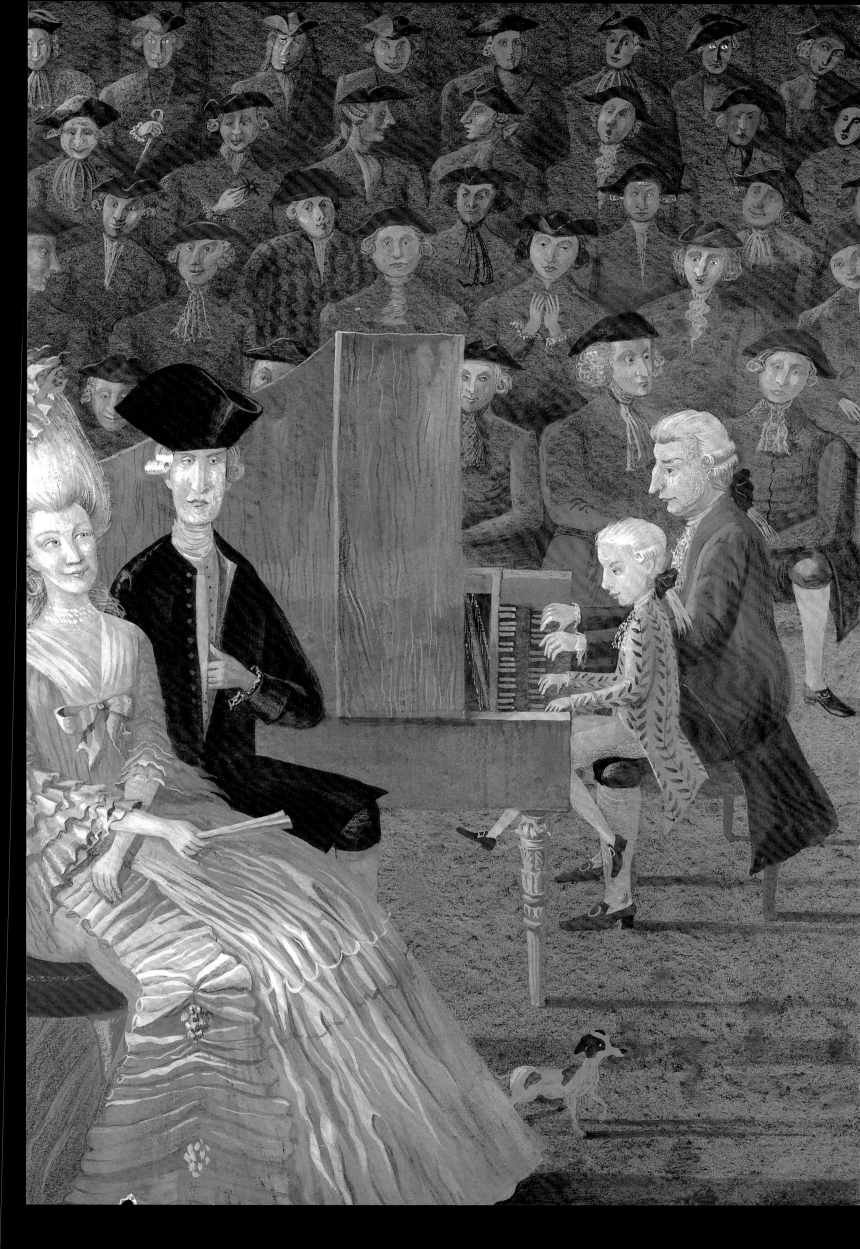

After being on the road for three and a half
years, it was only on the journey home that young
Mozart fell ill. He recovered in time to celebrate
his 12th birthday. However, soon after that he
completed his first opera. This long cherished dream
realized, he made a new wish. He wanted to visit
Italy, the home of opera.

This wish came true too.

Mozart and his father set off for Italy, arriving in the carnival season. The cities were bursting with life and activity and the streets were adorned with beautiful flowers and colorful lanterns. The people celebrated tirelessly, looking mysterious in their extraordinary masks and fine clothes. Fun-loving and excitable, Mozard was captivated.

Whenever he could, he would slip away at the end of a performance, put on a mask, and join the merrymakers in the street.

While in Italy, Mozart attended some performances of sacred music in the Sistine Chapel. After listening to this music, he went back and wrote an entire score from memory! This achievement made Italians admire him more than ever. They called him a messenger of God and his music the voice of the heavens. The Pope personally bestowed on him the Order of the Golden Spur. Mozart was the youngest person ever to receive this honor, but he wasn't impressed. He thought honors and awards were nonsense. They were useless for anything except to pin on your chest. Mozart's father, however, was very pleased.

Just as Mozart's fame was beginning to spread, he had to return home. This was the moment when Salzburg began to cast its shadow over Mozart's life.

The previous archbishop of Salzburg, Mozart's father's boss, had died. He had been a good and benevolent man; however, the new man had no love of music. He didn't want his musicians traveling around performing in other places either. So Mozart's father had no choice but to try to find Mozart a job in the court. The harshness and arrogance of his new boss, as well as the envy and spite of the other musicians, turned Salzburg into a prison for Mozart. It was only by remembering the happy times in his past and throwing himself into his music that Mozart could be free again. Music unlocked his cell door and allowed him to roam content.

Five years passed and Mozart was now a youth of 21. It was time to see the world again. This time, his father, who normally took charge of everything, couldn't leave his job. So Mozart happily set off with his mother. They went to Paris, but the fickle city didn't throw its arms open in welcome this time. The warmth with which it had received the child prodigy was gone. Instead, Mozart faced cold weather, chilly streets, and the Parisian's indifferent faces. He felt rejected and alone.

They rented a small apartment. In the daytime Mozart taught music in the homes of the rich and famous. At night, he was partying, leaving his worried mother alone, knitting and waiting in the damp, dark flat. During this time, Mozart wrote the famous *Paris Symphony,*

which the Parisians loved. That was one of the rare moments of brightness in an otherwise depressing and gloomy time. After his mother fell ill and died, Mozart silently left Paris.

After his return to Salzburg, Mozart yearned for freedom more than ever. He bitterly resented the way the archbishop treated him like a servant. After one argument with his father, he wrote to him, saying that anyone with a noble heart was a noble. Mozart was tired of self-important people around him, and he wasn't interested, as his father was, in seeking a noble position or title. He decided to move far away from Salzburg and begin a new life in Vienna.

In Vienna, he disobeyed his father once again by marrying Constanze Weber. They were married in St. Stephen's, and as the bells pealed out across the wide, blue skies, Mozart rejoiced in his happiness and his freedom.

Mozart and his wife were both outgoing and sociable people. After they were married, their house was always full of guests. Yet even when there were none, the house was rarely quiet. If their new baby boy Karl cried, the pet bird would join in, followed by the pet dog! Yet with all this going on, Mozart could still write. Alone in his own private, peaceful world of the imagination, he composed hour after hour of flawless music.

Mozart's music conquered the discerning Vienna audiences. Even the Emperor was an admirer. But here as elsewhere there were envious musicians who gathered like nasty clouds trying to prevent his sun from shining. As a result of their scheming, his opera, *The Marriage of Figaro,* was almost not performed. When it was performed, it was well received but quickly forgotten.

A year later, it opened again in Prague and was an enormous success.

After each performance, the audience
filled the hall with applause and flowers.
No one wanted to leave. Prague asked
him to write another opera, and he
immediately began work on *Don
Giovanni*. He was working on it when
his father died. Mozart and his father
had disagreed about many things and
were very different people. But Mozart
was a loyal and loving son, and the
death of his father, although it gave him
more freedom, was a terrible loss.

Mozart became a court musician in Vienna not long after his father died, something his father had always wanted. When *Don Giovanni* was performed there, the King said to him, "It's even better than *The Marriage of Figaro*, but I'm afraid the people won't know how to appreciate it."

Full of confidence, Mozart replied, "Give them time."

As a court musician, Mozart received a regular salary, but he never seemed to have enough money. He and his wife lived poorly, borrowing money from friends and moving from house to new house whenever their debts got too bad. Yet none of these worries ever influenced Mozart's music. He was writing very mature works, fresh and natural, lively but not too fancy.

One night, while Mozart was writing his next opera
The Magic Flute, a black-coated man appeared at his door and
asked Mozart to write a requiem for him. Since the man offered to
pay immediately, Mozart agreed. Despite illness, he worked constantly
on this requiem, often throughout the night, growing weaker with
each day. As his body grew weaker, his mind grew confused.
He began to believe that the black-coated man was the messenger
of Death and that the requiem he had ordered was for Mozart's own
funeral.

Mozart was buried on a cold, drizzly winter's day in 1791.
There was no coffin and no headstone. But his genius wasn't buried,
and his music lives on as pure, fresh, and refreshing as spring rain to
nourish the hearts of people everywhere, always.

BIOGRAPHY

Author Diane Cook is a journalist and freelance writer. She has written hundreds of newspaper articles and writes regularly for national magazines, trade publications, and web sites. She lives in Dover, Delaware, with her husband and three children.

English text copyright © 2003
Mason Crest Publishers, Inc.
All rights reserved.

Illustrations copyright © 2000
Art Agency "PIART"
Published in association with
Grimm Press Ltd., Taiwan

1 3 5 7 9 8 6 4 2

Library of Congress Cataloging-in-
Publication Data

On file at the Library of Congress

ISBN 1-59084-135-2